Published by 101 Private Tutors Ltd
101 Grange Drive, Melton Mowbray, .
First Edition: March 2016
ISBN–978-1530544493

Disclaimer

We have taken great care to ensure that the answers given on these cards are appropriate to the specified exams. However, we do not make any guarantee that the answers given here will always be awarded the maximum number of marks for any given exam question, as we have no control over the exam mark schemes. These Revision Cards do not constitute an entire revision programme, and should be used alongside other exam preparation materials. We do not take responsibility for the exam results of any person who uses these Revision Cards.

CONTENTS

About Revision Cards

Instructions

Common Mistakes

Inorganic Chemistry

1. Group 2: Alkaline Earth Metals
2. Reactions of Group 2 Metals
3. Group 7 – Halogens
4. Group 7 – Halides
5. Tests for Anions
6. Tests for Cations

Organic Chemistry

1. Naming Compounds: Terminology
2. Naming Compounds: Alkanes
3. Naming Compounds: Functional Groups
4. Formulae
5. Isomerism
6. Bonding in Organic Molecules
7. Reaction Mechanism Definitions
8. Types of Reactions
9. Reaction Mechanisms
10. Reactions of Alkanes
11. Reactions of Halogenoalkanes
12. Reactions of Alkenes
13. Reactions of Alcohols I
14. Reactions of Alcohols II
15. Analytical Techniques
16. Practical Techniques
17. Environmental Concerns

Revision Cards

We have painstakingly trawled through specifications, textbooks and exam mark schemes to produce these Revision Cards. Our own experiences of where students perform badly in exams have helped to ensure that these Revision Cards contain the most relevant facts to help you maximise your exam grades. There are key definitions, equations, reactions and other facts on these cards, all of which you need to learn off-by-heart.

Students who combine a comprehensive knowledge of the facts on these cards with a good understanding of Chemistry (and practise plenty of past papers) should be well on their way to achieving top grades.

We wish you success in your exams!

More Revision Cards

A full list of our Revision Cards can be found at: *www.RevisionTools.co.uk*

We are working hard to produce a range of Maths and Science Revision Cards for GCSE and A level across various exam boards. Our Revision Cards are also available as:

Printed Revision Cards   **Digital Book (Kindle & iBook stores)**

About Us

We are a small group of teachers, tutors and examiners who work for a tuition company called 101 Private Tutors Ltd. We have decades of combined teaching experience, thousands of hours of tuition experience and have marked many thousands of exam papers across a range of subjects as examiners/team leaders. We have come together to put our collective experiences into producing new GCSE and A level revision materials to help students avoid some of the common pitfalls in today's exams.

Contact

We would love to hear your suggestions, requests, criticisms and compliments:

contact@RevisionTools.co.uk

www.RevisionTools.co.uk

Instructions

You can use these Revision Cards however you wish, but you will probably find the following method particularly effective:

1) Choose a card – look at the title and instructions (do NOT look at the answers yet).

2) Try to write down the facts that the card asks for (the number in brackets tells you how many things you need to write down).

3) Compare the answers on the next page to what you have written.

4) Write out any corrections in a different colour.

5) Do this frequently for each card, but not more than once per day.

6) Practise the cards that you are struggling with more frequently than the ones that you find easy.

Some definitions are marked with a star (*): these should be learnt word–for–word.

Common Mistakes

Here are a few common mistakes that you should try to avoid:

Practising Too Often:

If you practise using these cards lots of time in one day then you will mostly be exercising your short-term memory. Try not to practise more than once per day, so that you exercise your long-term memory and remember things for longer.

Looking at the Answers:

It is very tempting to take a peek at the answers before you start, but this means that you only use your short-term memory. Do not look at the answers until you have tried writing them out to ensure that you build up your long-term memory.

Not Writing Down Answers:

Make sure you write down the answers each time so that you can check them against the card. If you just run through them in your head then you might not realise that you are making little mistakes.

Giving Up Too Quickly:

Sometimes you don't feel like you can remember any of the answers, or you are not certain that they are correct. Have a go anyway! Give yourself a minute to think about the topic and write down anything that comes to mind. Then check your answers. The process of trying to remember the answers will get your brain working and make learning easier.

Trying to Learn Too Much:

Don't try to do all of the cards in one sitting on your first attempt. Do a few cards on the first day and then add a few more each day until you are doing all of them. If you try to do all of them in your first go then you will get overwhelmed, so build it up a little bit at a time to make it easier.

1

Atoms & Elements

State the properties of subatomic particles.

Explain what the numbers on nuclear symbols mean.

Define *Element*, *Isotopes* and *Ion*.

Subatomic Particles:

Subatomic Particle	Relative Mass	Relative Charge
Proton	1	+1
Neutron	1	0
Electron	$\frac{1}{1836}$	-1

The plus and minus signs for the relative charges are **essential**

Nuclear Symbols:

$$^A_Z X$$

A = Mass Number (total number of protons and neutrons)
Z = Atomic Number (number of protons)

Element:

A group of atoms which all have the same number of protons

---

*Isotopes:

Atoms which have the same number of protons but a different number of neutrons

---

Ion:

An atom which has different numbers of protons and electrons, and hence has a positive or negative charge

Electronic Structure

Define *Orbital*.
What shape are orbitals?

How many electrons can each shell and sub-shell hold?

What order are the sub-shells filled in?

*Orbital:

An atomic orbital is a region within an atom that can hold up to 2 electrons with opposite spins

---

Shape of orbitals:

s: spherical

p: dumb-bell shaped

Maximum number of electrons per shell:

- 1st quantum shell: 2
- 2nd quantum shell: 8
- 3rd quantum shell: 18
- 4th quantum shell: 32

Sub-shell occupancy:

- s: 2 electrons (i.e. 1 orbital)
- p: 6 electrons (i.e. 3 orbitals)
- d: 10 electrons (i.e. 5 orbitals)
- f: 14 electrons (i.e. 7 orbitals)

You can deduce this from the periodic table

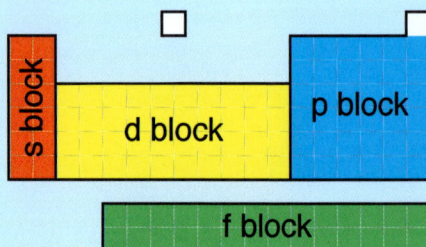

Sub-shell order:

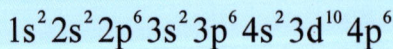

$$1s^2 2s^2 2p^6 3s^2 3p^6 4s^2 3d^{10} 4p^6$$

You can deduce this from the periodic table too

Transition Metals:

- **Filling:** 3d fills **after** 4s *(as per sub-shell order above)*

- **Exceptions:** Chromium and Copper only have one electron in the 4s sub-shell

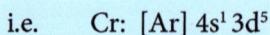

  i.e.   Cr: [Ar] $4s^1 3d^5$ Cu: [Ar] $4s^1 3d^{10}$

Equations for Chemical Calculations

State the 8 equations that you need to know for chemical calculations.

State units for all quantities.

Avogadro Constant:

$$\text{Number of Moles (mol)} = \frac{\text{Number of Particles}}{\text{Avogadro Constant}} \qquad n = \frac{N}{L}$$

Calculating Moles:

$$\text{Number of Moles (mol)} = \frac{\text{Mass (g)}}{\text{Molar Mass (g mol}^{-1})} \qquad n = \frac{m}{M_r}$$

Concentration:

$$\text{Concentration (mol dm}^{-3}) = \frac{\text{Number of Moles (mol)}}{\text{Volume (dm}^3)} \qquad c = \frac{n}{V}$$

$$\text{Concentration (g dm}^{-3}) = \frac{\text{Mass (g)}}{\text{Volume (dm}^3)} \qquad c = \frac{m}{V}$$

Important: *Volumes given in cm³ must be converted to dm³ by dividing by 1000*

Important: *Pay careful attention to which units are used for concentration in each question*

Gas Volume:

$$\text{Number of Moles (mol)} = \frac{\text{Volume (dm}^3)}{\text{Molar Gas Volume (dm}^3)} \qquad n = \frac{V}{V_m}$$

Important: *Volumes given in cm³ must be converted to dm³ by dividing by 1000*

Ideal Gas Equation:

$$PV = nRT$$

*P = Pressure (in Pascals, Pa or Nm⁻²), V = Volume (**in m³**), n = number of moles,*
T = Temperature (in Kelvin, K), R = Ideal Gas Constant (value provided on data sheet)

Percentage Yield:

$$\text{Percentage Yield} = \frac{\text{Actual Yield}}{\text{Theoretical Yield}} \times 100$$

Ensure the actual and theoretical yields are in the same units

Atom Economy:

$$\text{Atom Economy (\%)} = \frac{\text{Molecular Mass of Desired Products}}{\text{Sum of Molecular Masses of All Products}} \times 100$$

Pay close attention to units, particularly for volumes.
Remember: 1 m³ = 1000 dm³ = 1,000,000 cm³

Energetics Equations

State the 2 equations that you need to know
for energetics calculations.

State units for all quantities.

Heat of Reaction:

$$Q = mc\Delta T$$

IMPORTANT:

Q = heat given out or taken in by the chemical reaction (in Joules, J)
m = mass (in grams, g) of the substance being heated up (usually water)
c = specific heat capacity (which will be given in the question)
ΔT = change in temperature (in °C or K)

Note: If you are asked to calculate $\Delta_r H$ or $\Delta_c H$ then divide Q by the number of moles reacted/combusted

Also Note: If you have added a solid to water then the mass (m) is the total mass of the water plus the solid

---

Enthalpy Change of Reaction:

$$\text{Enthalpy Change of Reaction} = \sum \left(\begin{array}{c} \text{Bond Enthalpies} \\ \text{of Reactants} \end{array} \right) - \sum \left(\begin{array}{c} \text{Bond Enthalpies} \\ \text{of Products} \end{array} \right)$$

Make sure that you understand this notation and know how to use this equation

Masses & Formulae

Define *Relative Atomic Mass*, *Relative Molecular Mass*, *Relative Isotopic Mass* and *Relative Formula Mass*.

Define *Molecular Formula* and *Empirical Formula*.

*Relative Atomic Mass (A_r):

> The weighted mean mass of an atom of an element relative to one twelfth of the mass of an atom of carbon–12

*Relative Molecular Mass (M_r):

> The mass of a molecule relative to one twelfth of the mass of an atom of carbon–12

Relative Isotopic Mass:

> The mass of an atom of an isotope relative to one twelfth of the mass of an atom of carbon–12

Relative Formula Mass (M_r):

> The mass of a formula unit (of a giant structure) relative to one twelfth of the mass of an atom of carbon–12

Molecular Formula:

> Shows the actual number of atoms of each element in the molecule
> e.g. $C_4H_{10}O_2$

*Empirical Formula:

> Shows the simplest whole number ratio of atoms of each element in the compound
> e.g. C_2H_5O

Common Molecules, Ions, Acids and Bases

State the formulae of 4 molecules, 8 ions, 2 acids and 3 bases that you should know.

Molecules:

Water	H_2O
Carbon Dioxide	CO_2
Oxygen	O_2
Chlorine (or any halogen)	$Cl_2\ (X_2)$

Anions:

Chloride ion (or any halide ion)	$Cl^-\ (X^-)$
Hydroxide ion	OH^-
Sulfate ion	SO_4^{2-}
Carbonate ion	CO_3^{2-}
Nitrate ion	NO_3^-
Cyanide ion	CN^-

Cations:

Silver ion	Ag^+
Ammonium ion	NH_4^+

Acids:

Hydrochloric Acid	HCl
Sulfuric Acid	H_2SO_4

Bases:

Sodium Hydroxide	$NaOH$
Potassium Hydroxide	KOH
Ammonia (weak base)	NH_3

7

Oxidation & Reduction: Redox

State 4 different ways of describing oxidation and reduction.

Define *Disproportionation*.

What are *Reducing Agents* and *Oxidising Agents*?

What do the Roman numerals in formulae denote?

Oxidation & Reduction:

Oxidation	Reduction
Increase in Oxidation Number	Decrease in Oxidation Number
Loss of electrons	Gain of electrons
Addition of Oxygen	Loss of Oxygen
Loss of Hydrogen	Addition of Hydrogen

These are all good ways to figure out whether something has been oxidised or reduced, but if lots of them are happening at once then the only reliable one to look at is the Oxidation Number

Disproportionation:

Disproportionation occurs when a species is simultaneously oxidised and reduced to form two different products

Oxidising Agent, [O]:

A compound which oxidises another compound (by gaining electrons and hence being reduced in the process)

Reducing Agent, [H]:

A compound which reduces another compound (by losing electrons and hence being oxidised in the process)

Formulae:

Roman Numerals indicate the oxidation number of the named element. e.g.
- iron (II) – iron has an oxidation number of 2 (Fe^{2+})
- iron (III) – iron has an oxidation number of 3 (Fe^{3+})
- chlorate (I) – chlorine has an oxidation number of 1 (ClO^-)
- chlorate (III) – chlorine has an oxidation number of 3 (ClO_2^-)

Note: Compounds with –ate in the name also contain oxygen, but the roman numeral refers to the named element i.e. chlorine in this case

You **must** learn how to determine oxidation states

Ionic Bonding

What is *Ionic Bonding*?
What type of elements bond ionically?

What structure do ionic materials form?
Draw a diagram.

How is Ionic Bond Strength affected by ionic
charge and ionic radius?

Describe the properties of ionic materials.

*Ionic Bonding:

The strong electrostatic attraction between oppositely charged ions

Occurrence:

Ionic Bonding occurs between metals and non-metals

Structure:

Giant Ionic Lattice – Regular arrangement of oppositely charged ions

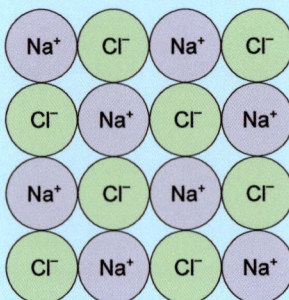

Ionic Bond Strength:

- Increases as ionic charge increases
- Decreases as ionic radius increases

Electrical Conductivity:

Solid: Does not conduct electricity – ions are fixed in lattice

Liquid (Molten): Conducts electricity – ions are mobile

Aqueous (Dissolved): Conducts electricity – ions are mobile

Melting and Boiling Points:

High melting and boiling points – a large amount of energy is required to overcome the strong electrostatic attraction between oppositely charged ions

Solubility:

Tend to be soluble in water – polar water molecules break apart the ionic lattice

Metallic Bonding

What is *Metallic Bonding*?
What type of elements bond metallically?

What structure do metals form?
Draw a diagram.

Describe the properties of metals.

*Metallic Bonding:

The strong electrostatic attraction between cations (positive metal ions) and delocalised electrons

Occurrence:

Between metals

Structure:

Giant Metallic Lattice

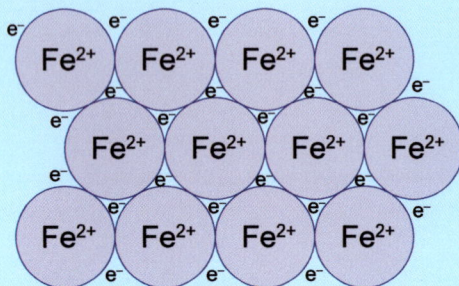

Electrical Conductivity:

Solid: Conducts electricity – delocalised electrons are mobile

Liquid (Molten): Conducts electricity – delocalised electrons are mobile

Melting and Boiling Points:

High melting and boiling points – a large amount of energy is required to overcome the strong electrostatic attraction between cations and delocalised electrons

Solubility:

Insoluble in water

Covalent Bonding

What is a *Covalent Bond*?
What is a *Dative Covalent Bond*?
What type of elements bond covalently?

What structures do covalent materials form?

Describe the properties of covalent materials.

*Covalent Bond:

The strong electrostatic attraction between a shared pair of electrons and the nuclei of the bonded atoms

*Dative Covalent (Co–ordinate) Bond:

A covalent bond where both electrons are donated by one of the atoms

Occurrence:

Between non-metals

Structures:

- Simple Molecular
- Giant Covalent Lattice

Electrical Conductivity:

Simple Molecular: Do not conduct electricity when solid, molten or aqueous – no mobile charge carriers

Giant Covalent Lattice: Most do not conduct electricity when solid or molten – no mobile charge carriers

Melting and Boiling Points:

Simple Molecular: Melting and boiling points (which are usually low) are determined by intermolecular forces

Giant Covalent Lattice: High melting and boiling points – a large amount of energy is required to overcome the many strong covalent bonds

Solubility:

Simple Molecular: Solubility in water determined by structure – polar molecules or molecules which form hydrogen bonds (e.g. alcohols) tend to be more soluble

Giant Covalent Lattice: Insoluble in water

Covalent Lattices

Describe the structures of *Diamond*, *Silicon* and *Graphite*.

Describe the structures of solid *Water* and *Iodine*.

Explain in detail the interactions between
the atoms/molecules.

Giant Covalent Lattices (Macromolecular Structures):

Regular arrangement of **atoms**

Held together by **strong covalent bonds**

Diamond (Carbon)/Silicon:

- Each atom bonds to 4 atoms
- Atoms form tetrahedral shape

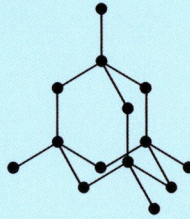

Graphite (Carbon):

- Each atom bonds to 3 atoms
- Atoms form trigonal planar shape
- Delocalised electrons between layers (allowing it to conduct electricity)
- Layers held together by London forces
- Single layer is called "Graphene"

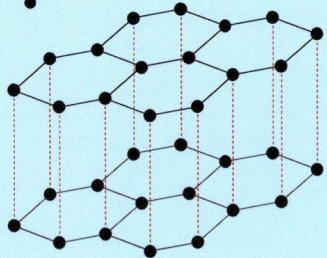

Silicon dioxide (SiO$_2$) *also forms a Giant Covalent Lattice.*

Simple Molecular Lattices:

- Regular arrangement of **molecules**
- Molecules are held together by **intermolecular forces**
- Lattice melts (I$_2$ sublimes) when intermolecular forces are overcome

Note: *Atoms **within** molecules are held together by strong covalent bonds; these do NOT break when it melts*

Ice (Water):

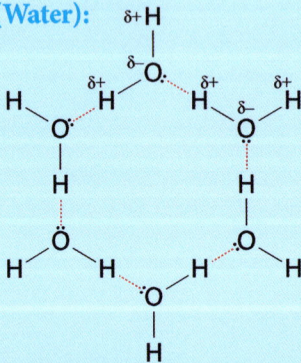

Held together by **Hydrogen bonds**

Ice has a lower density than water because the hydrogen bonds hold the molecules in an open lattice

Iodine:

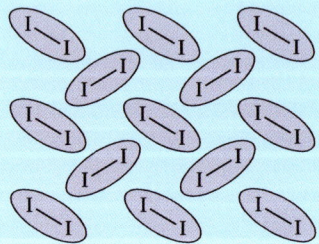

Held together by **London forces**

Intermolecular Forces

Where do intermolecular forces occur?

Name and define the 3 types of intermolecular force.

Define *Electronegativity*, *Dipole* and *Permanent Dipole*.

Occurrence:

Intermolecular forces occur in covalent materials with simple molecular structures

---

*London forces (instantaneous dipole–induced dipole forces):

The weak attractive force between an instantaneous dipole and an induced dipole in a neighbouring molecule

---

*Permanent dipole–permanent dipole forces:

The attractive force between permanent dipoles in neighbouring molecules

---

*Hydrogen bond:

A strong dipole–dipole attraction between an electron deficient hydrogen atom (in −OH, −NH or HF) and a lone pair of electrons on a highly electronegative atom (O, N or F) in a neighbouring molecule

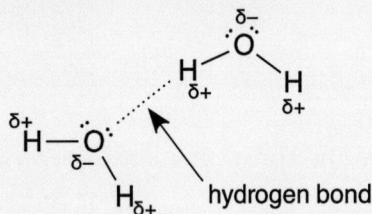

---

*Electronegativity:

The power of an atom to attract the electrons in a covalent bond

---

*Dipole/Polar bond/Polar molecule:

A covalent bond or molecule where the electron density is shifted more towards one end than the other

A molecule will only be polar if there are dipoles that do not cancel out (because the molecule is asymmetrical)

---

*Permanent dipole:

A permanent dipole is a small charge difference across a bond that results from a difference in the electronegativities of the bonded atoms

Boiling Points

Describe and explain how boiling point is affected by size, chain length, branching and functional group.

London forces (instantaneous dipole–induced dipole forces):

Size:

Larger atoms have more electrons, so the London forces are stronger

Chain Length:

Longer carbon chains result in more points of contact between the molecules, so the London forces are stronger

Branching:

Branched chains have fewer points of contact than straight chains, and the molecules cannot get as close to one another, leading to weaker London forces

Effect of London forces on Boiling Point:

Molecules with stronger London forces will have higher boiling points *(assuming all other intermolecular forces are the same)*

Hydrogen Bonding:

Functional groups:

Molecules containing O—H bonds cause hydrogen bonding (as do N—H bonds and H—F bonds)

Effect of Hydrogen Bonding on Boiling Point:

Molecules with hydrogen bonds will have higher boiling points than molecules without hydrogen bonds *(assuming the London forces are approximately the same)*

Explanation:

It takes more energy to overcome stronger intermolecular forces, so molecules with stronger intermolecular forces (i.e. hydrogen bonding or stronger London forces) will have higher boiling points

Important: *Water has higher melting and boiling points than expected for a group 6 hydride, because water is the only one that forms hydrogen bonds*

You may be asked to compare two or more molecular compounds and explain which has a higher boiling point. You should discuss all of the factors above that are applicable to the molecules in question.

Solvents and Solubility

What are *Polar Solvents* and *Non-Polar Solvents*?
Give examples.

What determines the solubility of compounds?
Discuss solubility in water and non-polar solvents.

Polar Solvents:

Molecules with a significant permanent dipole, e.g.
- Water (forms hydrogen bonds)
- Propanone (forms permanent dipole–permanent dipole interactions)

Non–Polar Solvents:

Molecules with no dipole/very weak dipole, e.g.
- Hexane (held together by London forces)

Solubility:

Molecules dissolve well if their intermolecular forces are a similar strength and type to those of the solvent

Solubility in Water:

Ionic substances
- Many dissolve well in water
- Ions become hydrated (surrounded by water molecules with their oppositely charged ends pointing at the ion)
- If ionic bonding is too strong then the ionic compound will not dissolve (as ions cannot be pulled out of lattice)

Alcohols
- Short-chain alcohols dissolve well in water
- OH group in alcohol forms hydrogen bonds with water
- Hydrocarbon chain is non-polar so it does not interact with water (so longer alcohols are less soluble)

Halogenoalkanes
- Do not dissolve in water
- Permanent dipoles in halogenoalkanes are much weaker than hydrogen bonds in water, so they do not interact with each other

Solubility in Non–Polar Solvents:

Non-polar molecules dissolve well in non-polar solvents because they form the same type of intermolecular force (i.e. London forces)

Shapes

What shapes can molecules form?
Draw an example of each, stating its name and bond angles.

Why do molecules form these shapes?

	Linear 2 bonds: 180° $O = C = O$ $Cl - Be - Cl$	2 electron pairs
	Trigonal Planar 3 bonds: 120° 	3 electron pairs

Tetrahedral 4 bonds: 109.5° 	**Trigonal Pyramidal** 3 bonds, 1 lone pair: 107° 	**Non-linear/Bent** 2 bonds, 2 lone pairs: 104.5° 	4 electron pairs

These are based on the tetrahedral structure, but each lone pair causes a 2.5° decrease in bond angle

Explanation: The electrons in bonds and lone pairs repel each other so that they spread out as much as possible	**Trigonal Bipyramidal** 5 bonds: 120° and 90° 	5 electron pairs
Repulsion: Lone pair–lone pair repulsions are stronger than lone pair–bonding pair repulsions, which are stronger than bonding pair–bonding pair repulsions	**Octahedral** 6 bonds: 90° 	6 electron pairs

Enthalpy Change Definitions

Define *Enthalpy Change*.

Define the 4 *Standard Enthalpy Changes*.

What are *Standard Conditions* and *Standard States*?

Define *Bond Enthalpy* and *Mean Bond Enthalpy*.

*Enthalpy Change, ΔH:

The heat energy change of a reaction measured at a constant pressure

If the "standard" symbol, $^\ominus$, is shown then the enthalpy change was also measured under standard conditions and substances were in their standard states

---

*Standard Enthalpy Change of Reaction, $\Delta_r H^\ominus$:

The enthalpy change when a reaction occurs in the molar quantities shown in the chemical equation, under standard conditions

---

*Standard Enthalpy Change of Formation, $\Delta_f H^\ominus$:

The enthalpy change when one mole of a compound is formed from its constituent elements in their standard states, under standard conditions

---

*Standard Enthalpy Change of Combustion, $\Delta_c H^\ominus$:

The enthalpy change when one mole of a substance is burned completely in oxygen, under standard conditions

---

*Standard Enthalpy Change of Neutralisation, $\Delta_{neut} H^\ominus$:

The enthalpy change when an acid reacts with an alkali to form one mole of water, under standard conditions

---

*Standard Conditions:

A pressure of 100 kPa and a specified temperature (usually 298 K)

e.g. $\Delta_r H^\ominus_{298}$ indicates that the enthalpy change was measured at a pressure of 100 kPa and a temperature of 298 K

Standard States:

The physical states of substances under standard conditions

Bond Enthalpy:

The energy required to break one mole of the specified bond in gaseous molecules

---

Mean Bond Enthalpy:

The bond enthalpy averaged over many different compounds

Bond enthalpy can be considered to be a measure of bond strength

Enthalpy Changes

Explain the following terms:
- *Exothermic*
- *Endothermic*
- *Activation Energy*

Draw Enthalpy Level Diagrams and Reaction Profile Diagrams for exothermic and endothermic reactions.

State Hess' Law.

Exothermic Reactions:

Give out energy (ΔH is negative)   *Bond making is exothermic*

Endothermic Reactions:

Take in energy (ΔH is positive)   *Bond breaking is endothermic*

Enthalpy Level Diagrams:

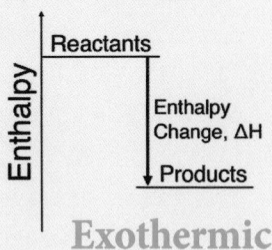

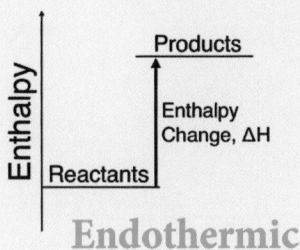

*Activation Energy:

The minimum energy required for a collision to result in a reaction

Reaction Profile Diagrams:

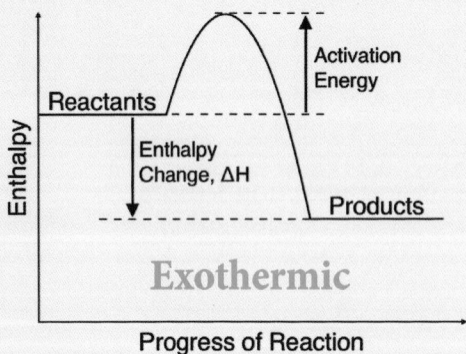

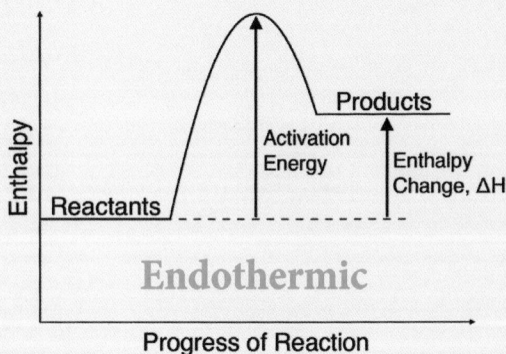

The Activation Energy and Enthalpy Change arrows must be drawn in the correct directions, as shown

Hess' Law:

The total enthalpy change for a reaction is always the same, no matter which chemical route is taken

*It is **REALLY** important that you can use Hess cycles – practise them!*

Rates of Reaction I

Define *Rate of Reaction*.
How can the rate of reaction be calculated?

How is the rate of reaction affected by temperature?
Draw a Boltzmann distribution showing this.

Rate of Reaction:

The change in concentration of a reactant or product over time

Calculating Rate of Reaction (equation):

$$\text{Rate of Reaction} = \frac{\text{Change in Concentration of Reactant (or Product)}}{\text{Time}}$$

Calculating Rate of Reaction (graphically):

Measure the gradient of a concentration versus time graph

If the graph is not a straight line then draw a tangent to the graph at the time you require

Temperature:

Increasing the temperature makes the particles **move faster**…

…therefore they will collide more frequently…

…therefore there will be more successful collisions per second…

…therefore the rate of reaction increases

Temperature:

Increasing the temperature gives the particles **more energy**…

…therefore more of the particles have enough energy to exceed the activation energy…

…therefore a greater proportion of the collisions are successful…

…therefore the rate of reaction increases

Boltzmann distribution:

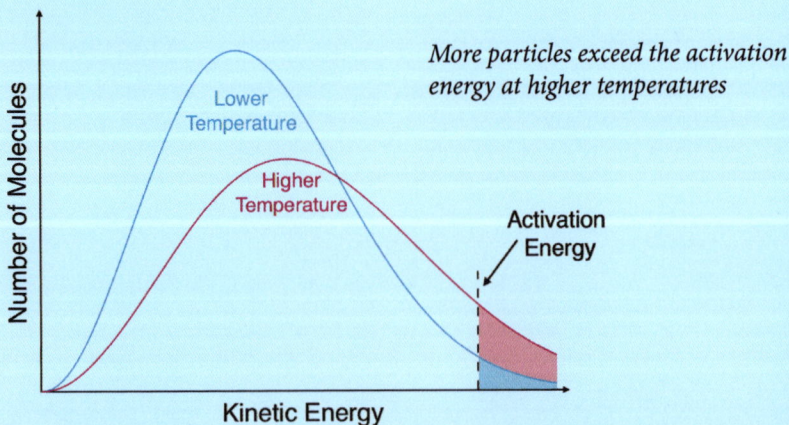

More particles exceed the activation energy at higher temperatures

Rates of Reaction II

How is the rate of reaction affected by pressure,
concentration and surface area?

Define *Catalyst*.

What is a *Homogeneous Catalyst*?
What is a *Heterogeneous Catalyst*?

Pressure/Concentration:

Increasing the pressure of a gas or concentration of a solution means that the particles are closer together...

...therefore the particles collide more frequently...

...therefore there will be more successful collisions per second...

...therefore the rate of reaction increases

Surface Area:

Increasing the surface area of a solid (often a catalyst) means that there are more sites where particles can collide with the surface...

...so there will be more collisions per second...

...therefore there will be more successful collisions per second...

...therefore the rate of reaction increases

*Catalyst:

Catalysts speed up a reaction without being chemically changed or used up by the overall reaction

Homogeneous Catalyst:

A catalyst which has the same physical state as the reactants

Usually aqueous or gaseous

Heterogeneous Catalyst:

A catalyst which has a different physical state from the reactants

Usually a solid catalyst with gaseous reactants, where the solid catalyst provides a surface for the gases to react on

20

Rates of Reaction III

How is the rate of reaction affected by catalysts?

Draw a Boltzmann Distribution and Reaction Profile Diagram to illustrate this.

Effect of Catalyst:

Catalysts provide an alternative reaction pathway...

...with a lower activation energy...

...so more particles exceed the activation energy...

...therefore a greater proportion of the collisions are successful...

...therefore the rate of reaction increases

Boltzmann Distribution:

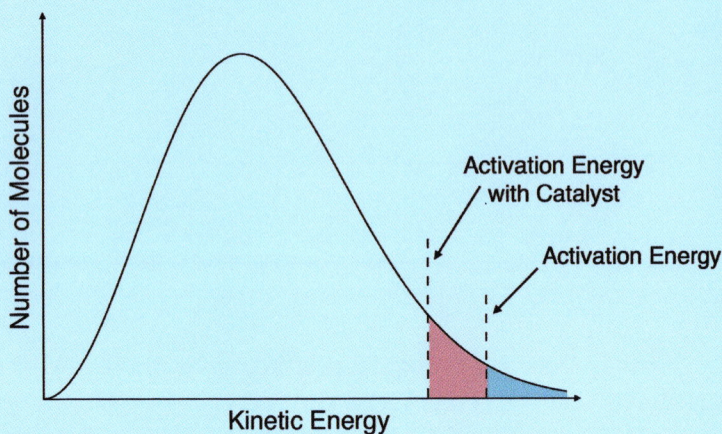

The activation energy has been lowered, so a greater proportion of the particles now exceed the activation energy

Reaction Profile Diagram:

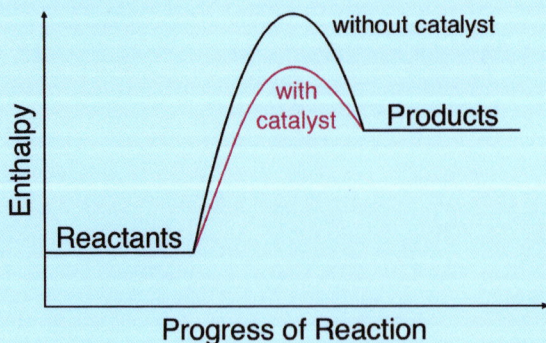

Equilibria

Define *Dynamic Equilibrium*.
State *Le Chatelier's Principle*.

Explain what happens to the equilibrium position when the temperature, pressure or concentration are changed, or when a catalyst is added.

*Dynamic Equilibrium:

A dynamic equilibrium exists in a closed system when the forward and reverse reactions are both occurring at the same rate, such that there is no overall change in the concentrations of the reactants or products

---

Le Chatelier's Principle:

When a system in dynamic equilibrium is subjected to a change, the equilibrium position will shift to minimise the change

---

Effect of Temperature:

Increasing the temperature causes the equilibrium position to move in the endothermic direction (in order to oppose the change and decrease the temperature), and vice versa

---

Effect of Pressure:

Increasing the pressure causes the equilibrium position to move in the direction of the side with the least gas molecules (in order to oppose the change and decrease the pressure), and vice versa

---

Effect of Concentration:

Increasing the concentration of a reactant causes the equilibrium position to move towards the products side (in order to oppose the change and decrease the concentration of the reactant), and vice versa

---

Effect of Catalyst:

Catalysts do not change the equilibrium position, but the reaction will reach equilibrium more quickly

---

Note: Temperature is the only factor which changes the value of the equilibrium constant

Equilibrium Constants

How do you calculate equilibrium constants for homogeneous and heterogeneous reactions?

Homogeneous Equilibrium Constant, K_c:

For homogeneous reactions (all products and reactants in same state):

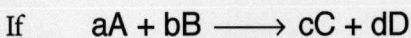

If $\quad$ aA + bB $\longrightarrow$ cC + dD

then $\quad K_c = \dfrac{[C]^c[D]^d}{[A]^a[B]^b}$

Heterogeneous Equilibrium Constant, K_c:

For heterogeneous reactions (reactants and/or products in different states):

Do not include solids and liquids in equilibrium constant equation (just write 1)

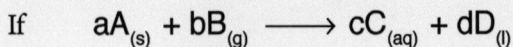

If $\quad$ aA$_{(s)}$ + bB$_{(g)}$ $\longrightarrow$ cC$_{(aq)}$ + dD$_{(l)}$

then $\quad K_c = \dfrac{[C]^c \times 1}{1 \times [B]^b}$

The larger the value of K_c, the further the equilibrium lies to the right

Periodicity

Define *Periodicity*.

What trends occur across periods and down groups?

Discuss the trends in melting and boiling points across periods.

*Periodicity:

The repeating pattern of trends in physical and chemical properties which occurs across different periods in the periodic table

Trends Across a Period:

- Nuclear Charge increases
- Shielding does not change significantly
- Atomic Radius decreases
- Therefore the Nuclear Attraction experienced by the outer electrons increases

Trends Down a Group:

- Nuclear Charge increases
- Shielding increases
- Atomic Radius increases
- Therefore the Nuclear Attraction experienced by the outer electrons decreases

Nuclear Charge and Shielding cancel each other out (approximately) so Atomic Radius is the dominant factor here

Melting and Boiling Points:

Melting and boiling points show similar (but complicated) trends across the different periods. These are based on chemical structure and bond strength (not nuclear charge, shielding and atomic radius).

You will need to use the ideas on this card to explain various trends such as ionisation energy, reactivity, electronegativity, reducing ability and thermal stability

Ionisation Energy

Define *First Ionisation Energy* and
Second Ionisation Energy, giving equations.

What factors affect ionisation energy?

What trends in ionisation energy occur across periods
and down groups?

*First Ionisation Energy:

The energy required to remove one electron from each atom in one mole of gaseous atoms to form one mole of gaseous 1+ ions

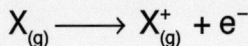

$$X_{(g)} \longrightarrow X^+_{(g)} + e^-$$

*You **must** include state symbols for ionisation energy equations*

*Second Ionisation Energy:

The energy required to remove one electron from each ion in one mole of gaseous 1+ ions to form one mole of gaseous 2+ ions

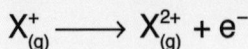

$$X^+_{(g)} \longrightarrow X^{2+}_{(g)} + e^-$$

Factors:

Factors affecting Ionisation Energy:
- Charge on the nucleus
- Distance (of the outer electrons) from the nucleus
- Electron shielding

You need to be able to explain the difference in ionisation energy between two elements in terms of these factors

Trend Across Period:

Ionisation energy increases across a period

Trend Down Group:

Ionisation energy decreases down a group

Group 2:
Alkaline Earth Metals

State the trend in reactivity of the Group 2 Metals.

State the trend in solubility of the
Group 2 Hydroxides and Sulfates.

State the trend in thermal stability of the
Group 2 Nitrates and Carbonates.

Compare these to thermal stability of the
Group 1 Nitrates and Carbonates.

Reactivity:

Increases down the group

You should explain this in terms of ionisation energies

Solubility of Group 2 Hydroxides, $M(OH)_2$:

Solubility **increases** down the group

Note: *$Mg(OH)_2$ is sparingly soluble*

Solubility of Group 2 Sulfates, MSO_4:

Solubility **decreases** down the group

Note: *$BaSO_4$ is insoluble*

Thermal Stability of Group 2 Nitrates and Carbonates:

Increases down the group

This is due to the increasing size and hence lower charge density of the cation (M^{2+}). This results in less polarisation of the anion, so the compound is more stable.

Thermal Stability of Group 1 Nitrates and Carbonates:

More stable than Group 2 Nitrates and Carbonates

This is due to the lower charge (M^+) and hence lower charge density of the cation. This results in less polarisation of the anion, so the compound is more stable.

Reactions of Group 2 Metals

Give equations for 6 reactions of Group 2 Metals
and their compounds.

Metal + Water:

Metal + Water $\longrightarrow$ Metal Hydroxide + Hydrogen

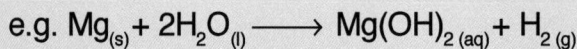

e.g. $Mg_{(s)} + 2H_2O_{(l)} \longrightarrow Mg(OH)_{2\ (aq)} + H_{2\ (g)}$

Metal + Oxygen:

Metal + Oxygen $\longrightarrow$ Metal Oxide

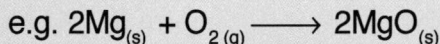

e.g. $2Mg_{(s)} + O_{2\ (g)} \longrightarrow 2MgO_{(s)}$

Metal + Chlorine:

Metal + Chlorine $\longrightarrow$ Metal Chloride

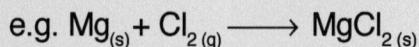

e.g. $Mg_{(s)} + Cl_{2\ (g)} \longrightarrow MgCl_{2\ (s)}$

Metal Oxide + Water:

Metal Oxide + Water $\longrightarrow$ Metal Hydroxide

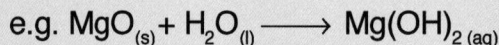

e.g. $MgO_{(s)} + H_2O_{(l)} \longrightarrow Mg(OH)_{2\ (aq)}$

Metal Oxide + Dilute Acid:

Metal Oxide + Acid $\longrightarrow$ Salt + Water

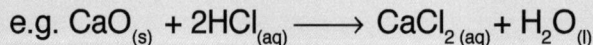

e.g. $CaO_{(s)} + 2HCl_{(aq)} \longrightarrow CaCl_{2\ (aq)} + H_2O_{(l)}$

Metal Hydroxide + Dilute Acid:

Metal Hydroxide + Acid $\longrightarrow$ Salt + Water

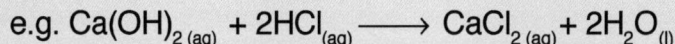

e.g. $Ca(OH)_{2\ (aq)} + 2HCl_{(aq)} \longrightarrow CaCl_{2\ (aq)} + 2H_2O_{(l)}$

3

Group 7 – Halogens

Give colours and states of halogens. Give colours of halogens when dissolved in water and in hexane.

State trends in 3 properties of halogens.

Give equations for 4 reactions of halogens.

Halogen colours:

Halogen	Colour		
	of element	in water	in hexane
Chlorine	yellow-green gas	pale green	pale green
Bromine	red-brown liquid	yellow-orange	orange-red
Iodine	grey crystals (purple vapour)	pale brown	violet

Melting & Boiling Points:

Melting & boiling points increase down the group

This is due to increased induced dipole–dipole forces (London forces) between the molecules

Reactivity:

Reactivity decreases down the group

You should explain this in terms of ease of forming 1– ions

Electronegativity:

Electronegativity decreases down the group

You should explain this in terms of how strongly the atom attracts electrons

Chlorine + Water:

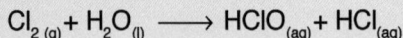

$$Cl_{2(g)} + H_2O_{(l)} \longrightarrow HClO_{(aq)} + HCl_{(aq)}$$

HClO is used to purify water (ClO$^-$ ions kill bacteria)

Chlorine + Cold Sodium Hydroxide:

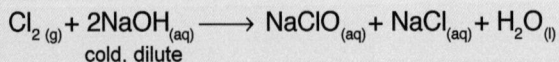

$$Cl_{2(g)} + 2NaOH_{(aq)} \longrightarrow NaClO_{(aq)} + NaCl_{(aq)} + H_2O_{(l)}$$
cold, dilute   *NaClO is bleach*

Halogen + Hot Alkali:

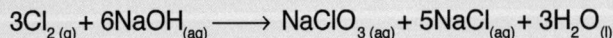

$$3Cl_{2(g)} + 6NaOH_{(aq)} \longrightarrow NaClO_{3(aq)} + 5NaCl_{(aq)} + 3H_2O_{(l)}$$

This reaction also works for other halogens and other alkalis

Halogen + Metal (Group 1 or Group 2):

Metal + Halogen $\longrightarrow$ Halide Salt

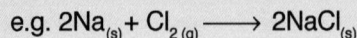

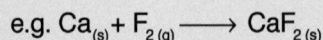

e.g. $2Na_{(s)} + Cl_{2(g)} \longrightarrow 2NaCl_{(s)}$

e.g. $Ca_{(s)} + F_{2(g)} \longrightarrow CaF_{2(s)}$

Group 7 – Halides

State the trend in Reducing Ability of Halide ions.

Give equations for reactions of halides with concentrated sulfuric acid.

Describe the displacement reactions of halide ions/halogens.

Give an equation for the reaction of hydrogen halides with ammonia.

Explain how hydrogen halides act as acids.

Reducing Ability of Halide Ions:

Reducing ability increases down the group

You should explain this in terms of how easily the halide ion loses electrons

---

Halides React with Concentrated Sulfuric Acid:

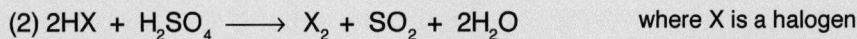

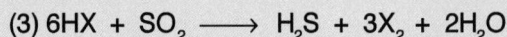

(1) $NaX + H_2SO_4 \longrightarrow NaHSO_4 + HX$

(2) $2HX + H_2SO_4 \longrightarrow X_2 + SO_2 + 2H_2O$ where X is a halogen

(3) $6HX + SO_2 \longrightarrow H_2S + 3X_2 + 2H_2O$

- All halides will react with concentrated sulfuric acid *(reaction 1)*
- Only bromide and iodide ions will reduce sulfur to SO_2 *(reaction 2)*
- Only iodide ions will further reduce sulfur to H_2S *(reaction 3)*

This is because the halide ions become stronger reducing agents further down the group

---

Displacement Reactions of Halides:

- Add a halogen to a halide ion solution
- Add hexane & shake
- If the halogen was more reactive than the halide ion then displacement occurs:

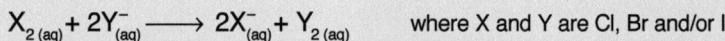

  $X_{2\,(aq)} + 2Y^-_{(aq)} \longrightarrow 2X^-_{(aq)} + Y_{2\,(aq)}$ where X and Y are Cl, Br and/or I

  (X must be more reactive than Y)
- Halide ions are colourless and dissolve in water, halogens dissolve in hexane
- Water and hexane will separate (hexane floats on water)

You need to be able to deduce which halide ion was present in a solution based on any colour changes that occur when it is mixed with chlorine, bromine or iodine. You need to use the order of the reactivity of the halogens in order to deduce which reactions will occur.

Hydrogen Halides React with Ammonia:

Hydrogen Halide + Ammonia $\longrightarrow$ Ammonium Salt

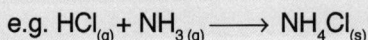

e.g. $HCl_{(g)} + NH_{3\,(g)} \longrightarrow NH_4Cl_{(s)}$

Hydrogen Halides are Acids:

Hydrogen halides dissolve in water and dissociate to form aqueous H^+ ions

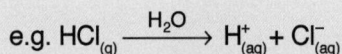

e.g. $HCl_{(g)} \xrightarrow{H_2O} H^+_{(aq)} + Cl^-_{(aq)}$

5

Tests for Anions

Describe tests for identifying:
- Carbonate ions
- Halide ions
- Hydroxide ions
- Sulfate ions

Anions:

Tests 1–3 must be performed in the sequence shown below:

1. Carbonate ions (CO_3^{2-}) and hydrogen carbonate ions (HCO_3^-):
- Add dilute acid

$$2H^+_{(aq)} + CO_3^{2-}{}_{(aq)} \longrightarrow CO_{2(g)} + H_2O_{(l)}$$
$$H^+_{(aq)} + HCO_3^-{}_{(aq)} \longrightarrow CO_{2(g)} + H_2O_{(l)}$$

- Bubble any gas evolved through limewater

Positive result: Carbon dioxide gas turns limewater cloudy

2. Sulfate ions (SO_4^{2-}):
- Add dilute hydrochloric acid (removes any carbonate/hydrogen carbonate ions)
- Add barium chloride solution

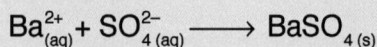

$$Ba^{2+}_{(aq)} + SO_4^{2-}{}_{(aq)} \longrightarrow BaSO_{4(s)}$$

Positive result: White precipitate of barium sulfate is formed

3. Halide ions (Cl^-, Br^-, I^-):
- Add dilute nitric acid
- Add silver nitrate solution – the colour of the precipitate formed indicates which halide ion is present

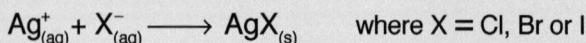

$$Ag^+_{(aq)} + X^-_{(aq)} \longrightarrow AgX_{(s)} \qquad \text{where } X = Cl, Br \text{ or } I$$

- Add ammonia solution – degree of solubility confirms the identity of the halide

Positive results:

Chloride ions: white precipitate, soluble in dilute ammonia

Bromide ions: cream precipitate, soluble in concentrated ammonia

Iodide ions: yellow precipitate, insoluble in ammonia

4. Hydroxide ions (OH^-):
- Dip a piece of red litmus paper into the solution

Positive result: Red litmus paper turns blue (because solution is alkaline)

6

Tests for Cations

Describe tests for identifying:
- Ammonium ions
- Group 1 and 2 ions

Ammonium ions (NH_4^+):

- Add sodium hydroxide solution
- Warm gently

$$NH_{4\ (aq)}^+ + OH_{(aq)}^- \longrightarrow NH_{3\ (g)} + H_2O_{(l)}$$

Positive result: Ammonia gas makes damp red litmus paper turn blue

---

Group 1 and 2 ions:

Flame Tests:

- Dip a loop of nichrome wire into concentrated hydrochloric acid
- Dip loop of wire into unknown compound
- Hold loop of wire in hot Bunsen burner flame

Positive results (flame colours):

Group 1	Lithium ions, Li^+	red
	Sodium ions, Na^+	orange/yellow
	Potassium ions, K^+	lilac
	Rubidium ions, Rb^+	red
	Caesium ions, Cs^+	blue
Group 2	Magnesium ions, Mg^{2+}	no colour
	Calcium ions, Ca^{2+}	brick red
	Strontium ions, Sr^{2+}	crimson
	Barium ions, Ba^{2+}	green

These colours are caused by electrons being excited into higher energy levels. When the electrons drop back down into lower energy levels they emit specific wavelengths of light characteristic of the energy levels in that element.

Naming Compounds: Terminology

Define the following terms:
- *Functional Group*
- *Homologous Series*
- *Hydrocarbon*
- *Alkyl group*
- *Aromatic/Arene*
- *Saturated*
- *Unsaturated*
- *Primary, Secondary, Tertiary*

*Functional Group:

A group of atoms responsible for the characteristic reactions of a compound

*Homologous Series:

A series of organic compounds with the same functional group where each successive member differs by CH_2

Hydrocarbon:

A compound containing **only** hydrogen and carbon atoms

Alkyl group:

A group derived from an alkane with one hydrogen atom missing, C_nH_{2n+1}

Aromatic/Arene:

A compound containing a benzene ring

Saturated:

A hydrocarbon with single carbon–carbon bonds only

Unsaturated:

A hydrocarbon containing double or triple carbon–carbon bonds (including aromatic rings)

Primary, Secondary, Tertiary:

Alcohols, halogenoalkanes and carbocations can be classified as either primary (1°), secondary (2°) or tertiary (3°). e.g. for alcohols:

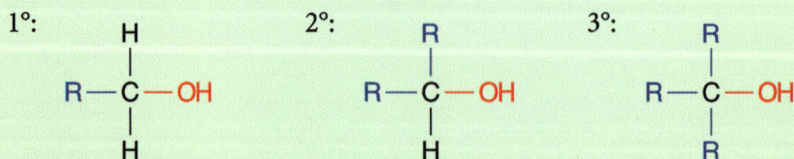

1°:
$$\begin{array}{c} H \\ | \\ R-C-OH \\ | \\ H \end{array}$$

2°:
$$\begin{array}{c} R \\ | \\ R-C-OH \\ | \\ H \end{array}$$

3°:
$$\begin{array}{c} R \\ | \\ R-C-OH \\ | \\ R \end{array}$$

1° alcohol has one R group attached to the carbon with the −OH group, 2° has two R groups, 3° has three R groups

Naming Compounds: Alkanes

Give the naming convention for straight chain alkanes, branched alkanes and cycloalkanes.
Give examples.

What is the General Formula for an alkane?

Name the first 10 straight chain alkanes.

| Alkanes: | –ane (e.g. propane) | $CH_3CH_2CH_3$ |

General Formula: C_nH_{2n+2}

This applies to straight chain and branched alkanes only

Straight chain alkanes:

	1 Carbon:	Methane
	2 Carbons:	Ethane
	3 Carbons:	Propane
	4 Carbons:	Butane
	5 Carbons:	Pentane
	6 Carbons:	Hexane
	7 Carbons:	Heptane
	8 Carbons:	Octane
	9 Carbons:	Nonane
	10 Carbons:	Decane

Branched alkanes: alkyl– –ane (e.g. methylpropane)

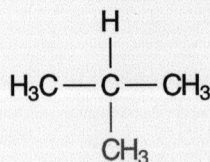

$$\begin{array}{c} H \\ | \\ H_3C - C - CH_3 \\ | \\ CH_3 \end{array}$$

Cycloalkanes: cyclo– –ane (e.g. cyclohexane)

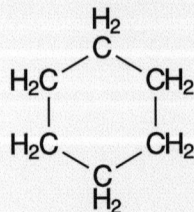

$$\begin{array}{ccc} & H_2 & \\ & C & \\ H_2C & & CH_2 \\ | & & | \\ H_2C & & CH_2 \\ & C & \\ & H_2 & \end{array}$$

3

Naming Compounds: Functional Groups

State the naming conventions for 8 functional groups.
Give an example of each.

Alkenes:	–ene (e.g. prop**ene**)	
General Formula:	C_nH_{2n}	

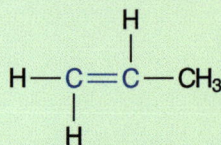

$$H-\underset{\underset{\displaystyle H}{|}}{\overset{\overset{\displaystyle H}{|}}{C}}=\underset{}{C}-CH_3$$

Halogenoalkanes:	chloro– –ane	
	bromo– –ane	
	iodo– –ane	
	e.g. 1–**bromo**pent**ane**	$CH_3CH_2CH_2CH_2CH_2Br$

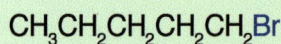

Alcohols:	–ol (e.g. ethan**ol**)	CH_3CH_2OH

Aldehydes: –al (e.g. propan**al**)

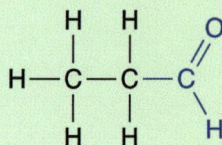

$$H-\underset{\underset{\displaystyle H}{|}}{\overset{\overset{\displaystyle H}{|}}{C}}-\underset{\underset{\displaystyle H}{|}}{\overset{\overset{\displaystyle H}{|}}{C}}-C\underset{\displaystyle H}{\overset{\displaystyle O}{\big<}}$$

Ketones: –one (e.g. propan**one**)

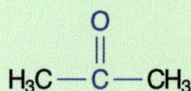

$$H_3C-\overset{\overset{\displaystyle O}{\|}}{C}-CH_3$$

Carboxylic Acids: –oic acid (e.g. ethan**oic acid**)

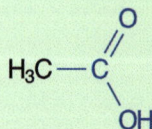

$$H_3C-C\underset{\displaystyle OH}{\overset{\displaystyle O}{\big<}}$$

Amines:	amino– (e.g. **amino**ethane)	
	–amine (e.g. ethyl**amine**)	

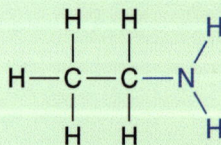

$$H-\underset{\underset{\displaystyle H}{|}}{\overset{\overset{\displaystyle H}{|}}{C}}-\underset{\underset{\displaystyle H}{|}}{\overset{\overset{\displaystyle H}{|}}{C}}-N\underset{\displaystyle H}{\overset{\displaystyle H}{\big<}}$$

Nitriles:	–nitrile (e.g. ethane**nitrile**)	$H_3C-C\equiv N$

Formulae

Explain the 6 types of chemical formula.
Give an example for each.

Molecular Formula:

Shows the actual number of atoms of each element in the molecule

e.g. $C_4H_{10}O_2$

---

*Empirical Formula:

Shows the simplest whole number ratio of atoms of each element in the compound

e.g. C_2H_5O

General Formula:

Shows the simplest algebraic formula for any member of a particular homologous series

e.g. $C_nH_{2n+1}OH$

Structural Formula:

Shows the minimum detail necessary to indicate the arrangement of the atoms in the molecule

e.g. $CH_3(CH_2)_2OH$

Displayed Formula:

Shows how the atoms are arranged and all of the bonds between the atoms.

e.g.

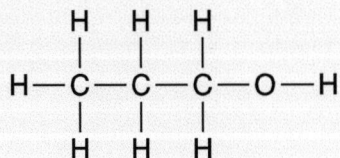

Skeletal Formula:

Shows only the bonds of the carbon skeleton and any functional groups. Carbon atoms are not shown, and neither are hydrogen atoms attached to carbon atoms.

e.g.

5

Isomerism

Explain what is meant by:
- *Structural Isomers*
- *Stereoisomers*
- *E–Z Isomerism*
- *Cis–Trans Isomerism*

How are E–Z isomers identified?
What causes E–Z isomerism?

*Structural Isomers:

Compounds with the same molecular formula but different structural formulae

Molecules can be unbranched/branched, the functional groups can be in different positions, or the functional groups may be different (e.g. aldehydes & ketones)

---

*Stereoisomers:

Compounds with the same structural formula but with a different arrangement of the atoms in space

---

E–Z Isomerism:

A type of stereoisomerism resulting from a $C=C$ group where each carbon atom has two different groups attached to it.

e.g.

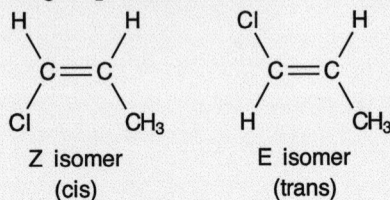

Z isomer
(cis)

E isomer
(trans)

Identifying E–Z Isomers:

Cahn-Ingold-Prelog (CIP) priority rules:
- E–isomer – two highest priority groups on opposite sides of double bond
- Z–isomer – two highest priority groups on the same side of the double bond

You need to learn the CIP rules so that you can identify E and Z isomers

---

Cause of E–Z Isomerism:

The lack of rotation about the $C=C$ double bond

Cis–Trans Isomerism:

A special case of E–Z isomerism in which the same group is found on both carbons in a $C=C$ double bond

Make sure that you can tell the difference between cis and trans isomers (see E–Z isomer diagram above)

6

Bonding in Organic Molecules

What are *σ-bonds* and *π-bonds*?

Draw a diagram to show how a π–bond is formed.

What shapes are commonly found in organic molecules?

σ–bonds:

- Single C—C and C—H bonds are called σ (sigma) bonds
- Formed by the overlap of orbitals directly between bonding atoms
- Free rotation

The high bond enthalpy and low polarity of the σ–bonds means alkanes are quite unreactive

---

π–bonds:

- The second bond in a C=C bond is called a π (pi) bond
- π–bonds can only form between two atoms if there is already a σ–bond
- Formed by the overlap of p–orbitals on adjacent double-bonding atoms
- Restricted rotation

The lower bond enthalpy of π bonds means that they break more easily, so alkenes are more reactive than alkanes

---

π–bonding diagram:

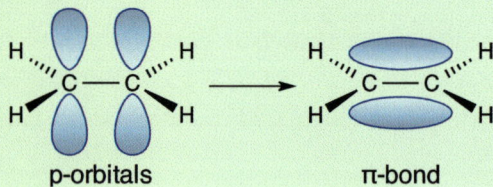

p-orbitals   π-bond

Shapes:

The shapes of organic molecules can be predicted using the rules for shapes on card **Blue 15** – use these rules to explain the following examples:

- **Tetrahedral** shape around C atom in alkanes (e.g. H—C—H or C—C—C, bond angle of 109.5°)
- **Trigonal planar** shape around C in alkenes (e.g. H—C—H or H—C=C, bond angle of about 120°)
- **Bent** shape around O atom in alcohols (e.g. C—O—H, bond angle of 104.5°)
- **Linear** shape around H atom in hydrogen bond (e.g. O—H----:O, bond angle of 180°)

You may also be asked to predict bond angles in more complex molecules

7

Reaction Mechanism Definitions

Define the following terms:
- *Electrophile*
- *Nucleophile*
- *Homolytic Fission*
- *Heterolytic Fission*
- *Radical*
- *Curly Arrow*

*Electrophile:

An electron pair acceptor

---

*Nucleophile:

An electron pair donor

---

*Homolytic Fission:

The breaking of a covalent bond, where one bonding electron goes to each atom, forming 2 radicals:

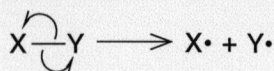

$$X\overset{\frown}{\underset{\smile}{-}}Y \longrightarrow X\bullet + Y\bullet$$

---

*Heterolytic Fission:

The breaking of a covalent bond, where both bonding electrons go to one of the atoms, forming a cation and an anion:

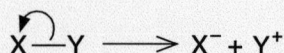

$$X\overset{\frown}{-}Y \longrightarrow X^- + Y^+$$

Radical:

A species with an unpaired electron

A single dot must be written next to the species to represent the unpaired electron, e.g. R•

Curly Arrow:

Represents the movement of a pair of electrons, showing either the formation or heterolytic fission of a covalent bond

8

Types of Reactions

Define the following terms:
- *Addition Reaction*
- *Substitution Reaction*
- *Elimination Reaction*
- *Oxidation Reaction*
- *Reduction Reaction*
- *Hydrolysis Reaction*
- *Polymerisation Reaction*

Addition Reaction:

A reaction in which a reactant is added to an unsaturated molecule to make a single product (2 reactants → 1 product)

Substitution Reaction:

A reaction in which an atom or group of atoms is replaced with a different atom or group of atoms (2 reactants → 2 products)

Elimination Reaction:

A reaction in which one molecule decomposes into two, where one is much smaller than the other (1 reactant → 2 products)

Oxidation Reaction:

A reaction in which a species loses one or more electrons

Reduction Reaction:

A reaction in which a species gains one or more electrons

Hydrolysis Reaction:

A reaction in which a molecule is split apart when it reacts with water

Polymerisation Reaction:

A reaction in which small simple molecules (monomers) are joined together to form a giant molecule (a polymer)

9

Reaction Mechanisms

Draw mechanisms for the following reactions:
- Free Radical Substitution
- Electrophilic Addition (2)
- Nucleophilic Substitution (2)

Free Radical Substitution:

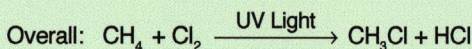

Overall: $CH_4 + Cl_2 \xrightarrow{\text{UV Light}} CH_3Cl + HCl$

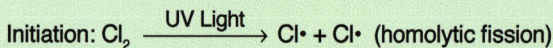

Initiation: $Cl_2 \xrightarrow{\text{UV Light}} Cl\cdot + Cl\cdot$ (homolytic fission)

*You may be asked to show
how this reaction mechanism
works with other alkanes or
with bromine*

Propagation:

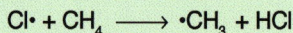

$Cl\cdot + CH_4 \longrightarrow \cdot CH_3 + HCl$

$\cdot CH_3 + Cl_2 \longrightarrow CH_3Cl + Cl\cdot$

Termination:

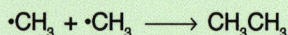

$Cl\cdot + \cdot CH_3 \longrightarrow CH_3Cl$

$\cdot CH_3 + \cdot CH_3 \longrightarrow CH_3CH_3$

Electrophilic Addition:

With Br₂:

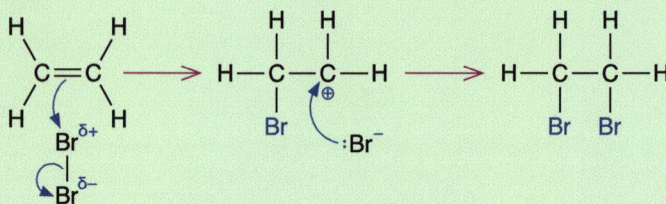

With HBr:

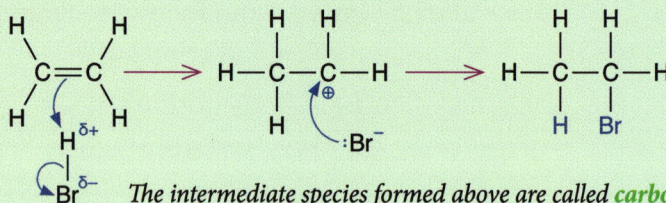

The intermediate species formed above are called carbocations

Nucleophilic Substitution:

With Aqueous OH⁻:

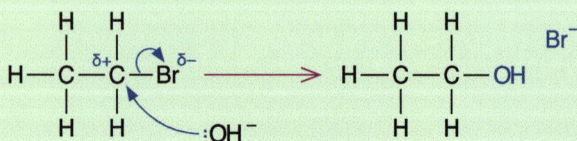

With Ethanolic NH₃:

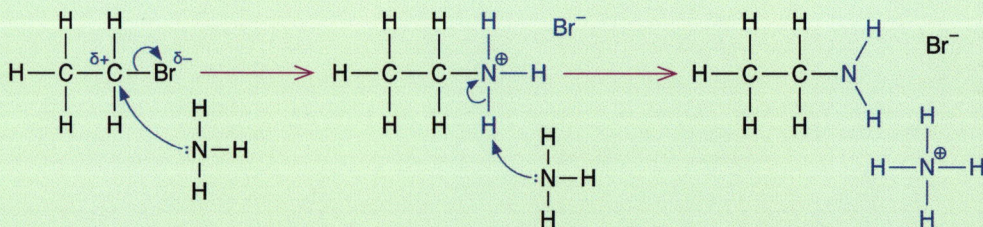

10

Reactions of Alkanes

Give equations for 5 reactions of alkanes.

Complete Combustion:

With sufficient oxygen alkanes undergo complete combustion:

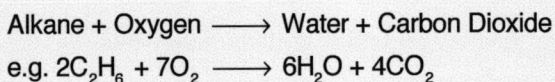

Alkane + Oxygen $\longrightarrow$ Water + Carbon Dioxide

e.g. $2C_2H_6 + 7O_2 \longrightarrow 6H_2O + 4CO_2$

Incomplete Combustion:

With insufficient oxygen alkanes undergo incomplete combustion:

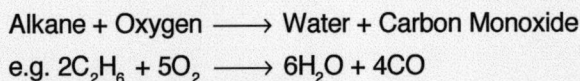

Alkane + Oxygen $\longrightarrow$ Water + Carbon Monoxide

e.g. $2C_2H_6 + 5O_2 \longrightarrow 6H_2O + 4CO$

Make sure that you can balance combustion equations. You may be asked to show how alkenes or alcohols combust – the basic reactions are same, but the numbers will be different.

Halogenation: *(mechanism required)*

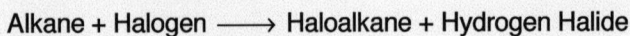

Alkane + Halogen $\longrightarrow$ Haloalkane + Hydrogen Halide

e.g. $CH_4 + Cl_2 \xrightarrow{\text{UV Light}} CH_3Cl + HCl$

This reaction is of limited use in synthesis as a mixture of organic products will be formed, particularly for longer chain alkanes

Cracking:

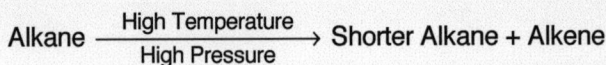

Alkane $\xrightarrow[\text{High Pressure}]{\text{High Temperature}}$ Shorter Alkane + Alkene

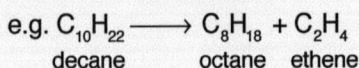

e.g. $C_{10}H_{22} \longrightarrow C_8H_{18} + C_2H_4$

decane   octane   ethene

Reforming:

Straight Alkane $\xrightarrow{\text{Catalyst}}$ Branched, Cyclic or Aromatic Hydrocarbon

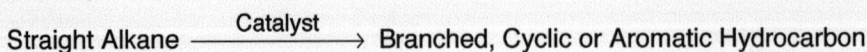

e.g. $CH_3(CH_2)_4CH_3 \longrightarrow$ ⬡ $+ H_2 \longrightarrow$ ⬢ $+ 4H_2$

hexane   cyclohexane   benzene

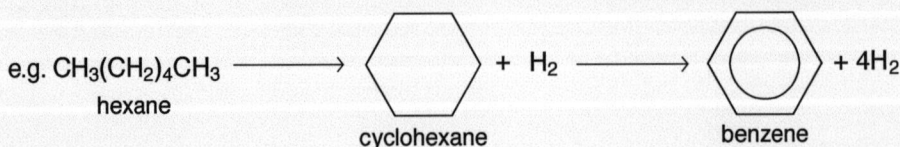

e.g. $CH_3(CH_2)_4CH_3 \longrightarrow CH_3CH(CH_3)CH_2CH_2CH_3$

hexane   2-methylpentane

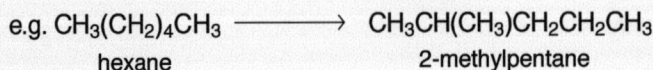

Branched and cyclic hydrocarbons combust more efficiently than straight-chain hydrocarbons

11

Reactions of Halogenoalkanes

Give equations for 5 reactions of halogenoalkanes.

Elimination with OH⁻:

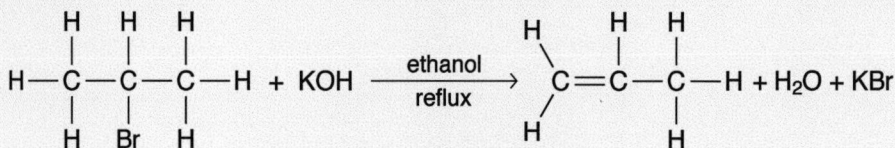

The OH⁻ ion is acting as a base (by accepting a proton)

Substitution with OH⁻: *(mechanism required)*

$$CH_3CH_2Br + NaOH \xrightarrow{\text{reflux}} CH_3CH_2OH + NaBr$$

Substitution with NH₃: *(mechanism required)*

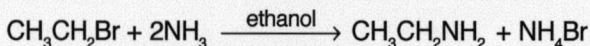

$$CH_3CH_2Br + 2NH_3 \xrightarrow{\text{ethanol}} CH_3CH_2NH_2 + NH_4Br$$

Substitution with CN⁻:

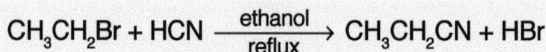

$$CH_3CH_2Br + HCN \xrightarrow[\text{reflux}]{\text{ethanol}} CH_3CH_2CN + HBr$$

This reaction allows chemists to increase the length of a carbon chain

---

Substitution with H₂O/Hydrolysis:

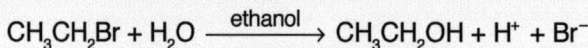

$$CH_3CH_2Br + H_2O \xrightarrow{\text{ethanol}} CH_3CH_2OH + H^+ + Br^-$$

The halogenoalkane is dissolved in ethanol (it is insoluble in water). We can compare the *rate of hydrolysis* of different halogenoalkanes by using aqueous AgNO₃ as the source of water and observing how quickly a precipitate forms:

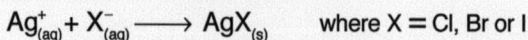

$$Ag^+_{(aq)} + X^-_{(aq)} \longrightarrow AgX_{(s)} \qquad \text{where X = Cl, Br or I}$$

The substitution reactions above can be performed with any halogenoalkane, but the rate of reaction will be determined by the carbon–halogen bond strength/enthalpy (faster reactions for weaker bonds) and the type of halogenoalkane (primary/secondary/tertiary).

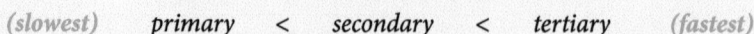

(slowest)   C—F < C—Cl < C—Br < C—I   *(fastest)*

(slowest)   *primary* < *secondary* < *tertiary*   *(fastest)*

In aqueous solutions some of the halogenoalkane will react with water producing an alcohol. The reagents must be dissolved in ethanol (e.g. ethanolic hydrogen cyanide) unless an alcohol is the desired product.

12

Reactions of Alkenes

Give equations for 6 reactions of alkenes.

Addition of Hydrogen:

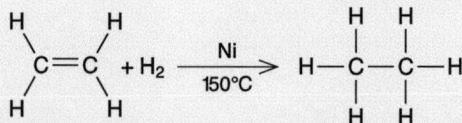

$$CH_2=CH_2 + H_2 \xrightarrow[150°C]{Ni} CH_3-CH_3$$

This reaction is used industrially to catalytically hydrogenate unsaturated vegetable oils to produce saturated hydrocarbons (e.g. margarine)

Addition of Hydrogen Halide: *(mechanism required)*

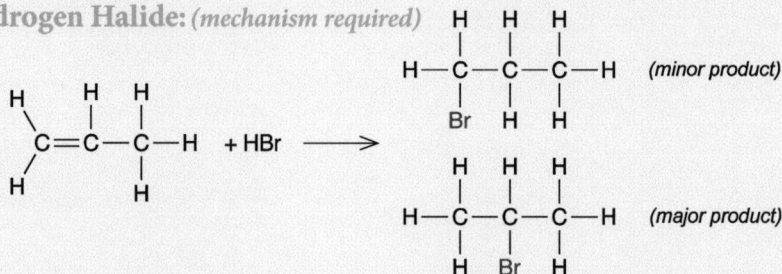

$$CH_2=CH-CH_3 + HBr \longrightarrow$$

H—C—C—C—H with Br on end carbon *(minor product)*

H—C—C—C—H with Br on middle carbon *(major product)*

Note: for unsymmetrical alkenes this reaction will produce two different isomers, according to *Markownikoff's Rule*:

The major product formed is where the hydrogen becomes attached to the carbon which already has the most hydrogens directly attached to it, as this forms the most stable carbocation intermediate

---

Addition of Halogen: *(mechanism required)*

Test for an Alkene:
Alkenes decolourise bromine water

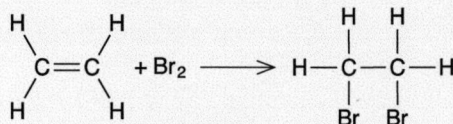

$$CH_2=CH_2 + Br_2 \longrightarrow BrCH_2-CH_2Br$$

Addition of Water (Steam):

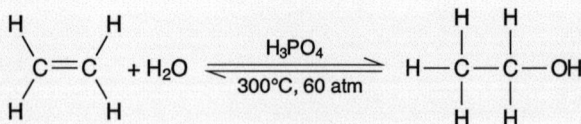

$$CH_2=CH_2 + H_2O \xrightleftharpoons[300°C, 60\ atm]{H_3PO_4} CH_3-CH_2-OH$$

Oxidation with Acidified Potassium Manganate (VII):

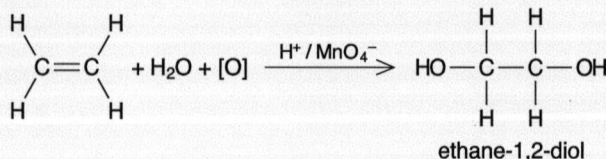

$$CH_2=CH_2 + H_2O + [O] \xrightarrow{H^+/MnO_4^-} HO-CH_2-CH_2-OH$$

ethane-1,2-diol

Addition Polymerisation:

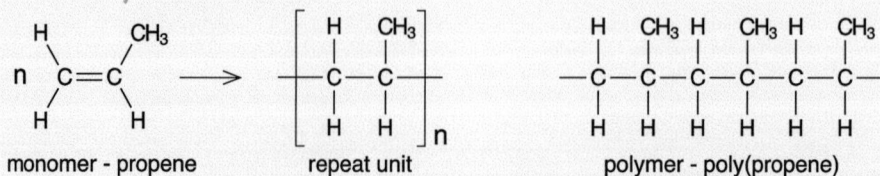

$$n\ CH_2=CH(CH_3) \longrightarrow \left[CH_2-CH(CH_3) \right]_n$$

monomer - propene   repeat unit   polymer - poly(propene)

13

Reactions of Alcohols I

Give 6 equations related to the oxidation of alcohols.

Oxidation of Primary Alcohols:

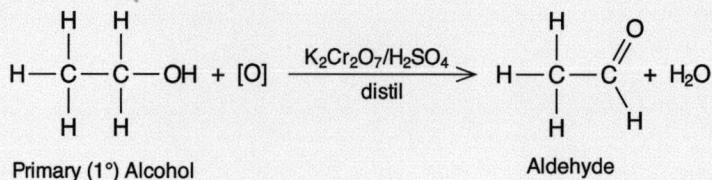

$$H-\overset{\overset{\displaystyle H}{|}}{\underset{\underset{\displaystyle H}{|}}{C}}-\overset{\overset{\displaystyle H}{|}}{\underset{\underset{\displaystyle H}{|}}{C}}-OH + [O] \xrightarrow[\text{distil}]{K_2Cr_2O_7/H_2SO_4} H-\overset{\overset{\displaystyle H}{|}}{\underset{\underset{\displaystyle H}{|}}{C}}-\overset{\displaystyle O}{\underset{\underset{\displaystyle H}{}}{C}} + H_2O$$

Primary (1°) Alcohol   Aldehyde

Further Oxidation of Primary Alcohols:

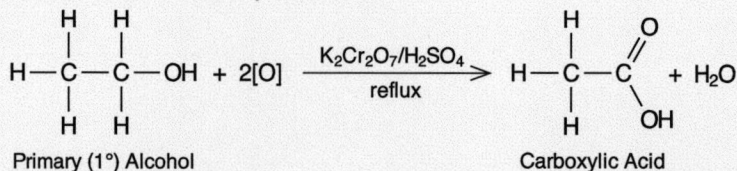

$$H-\overset{\overset{\displaystyle H}{|}}{\underset{\underset{\displaystyle H}{|}}{C}}-\overset{\overset{\displaystyle H}{|}}{\underset{\underset{\displaystyle H}{|}}{C}}-OH + 2[O] \xrightarrow[\text{reflux}]{K_2Cr_2O_7/H_2SO_4} H-\overset{\overset{\displaystyle H}{|}}{\underset{\underset{\displaystyle H}{|}}{C}}-\overset{\displaystyle O}{\underset{\underset{\displaystyle OH}{}}{C}} + H_2O$$

Primary (1°) Alcohol   Carboxylic Acid

Note the differences between these two reactions for primary alcohols (i.e. distil vs reflux)

Oxidation of Secondary Alcohols:

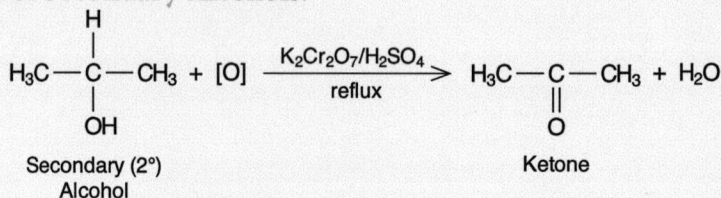

$$H_3C-\overset{\overset{\displaystyle H}{|}}{\underset{\underset{\displaystyle OH}{|}}{C}}-CH_3 + [O] \xrightarrow[\text{reflux}]{K_2Cr_2O_7/H_2SO_4} H_3C-\overset{}{\underset{\underset{\displaystyle O}{\|}}{C}}-CH_3 + H_2O$$

Secondary (2°)
Alcohol   Ketone

Oxidation of Tertiary Alcohols:

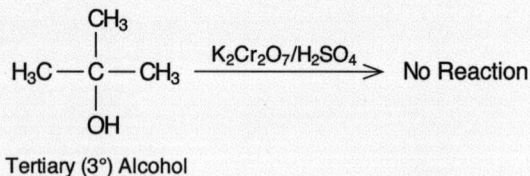

$$H_3C-\overset{\overset{\displaystyle CH_3}{|}}{\underset{\underset{\displaystyle OH}{|}}{C}}-CH_3 \xrightarrow{K_2Cr_2O_7/H_2SO_4} \text{No Reaction}$$

Tertiary (3°) Alcohol

Oxidation of Aldehydes:

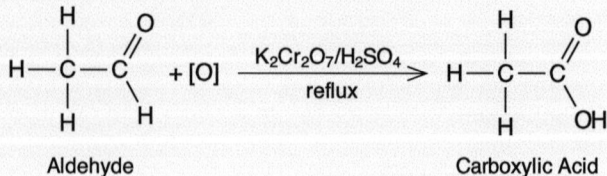

$$H-\overset{\overset{\displaystyle H}{|}}{\underset{\underset{\displaystyle H}{|}}{C}}-\overset{\displaystyle O}{\underset{\underset{\displaystyle H}{}}{C}} + [O] \xrightarrow[\text{reflux}]{K_2Cr_2O_7/H_2SO_4} H-\overset{\overset{\displaystyle H}{|}}{\underset{\underset{\displaystyle H}{|}}{C}}-\overset{\displaystyle O}{\underset{\underset{\displaystyle OH}{}}{C}}$$

Aldehyde   Carboxylic Acid

Test for an Aldehyde: Benedict's solution and Fehling's solution both turn from blue to red in the presence of an aldehyde (but not a ketone).

Oxidation of Ketones:

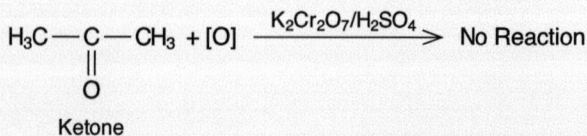

$$H_3C-\overset{}{\underset{\underset{\displaystyle O}{\|}}{C}}-CH_3 + [O] \xrightarrow{K_2Cr_2O_7/H_2SO_4} \text{No Reaction}$$

Ketone

14

Reactions of Alcohols II

Give equations for 5 reactions of alcohols.

Dehydration/Elimination of Water:

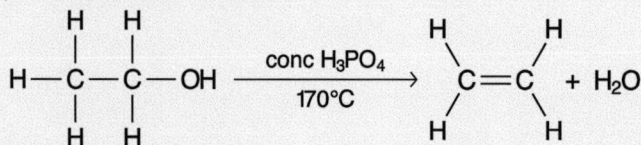

$$H-\underset{\underset{H}{|}}{\overset{\overset{H}{|}}{C}}-\underset{\underset{H}{|}}{\overset{\overset{H}{|}}{C}}-OH \xrightarrow[170°C]{conc\ H_3PO_4} \overset{H}{\underset{H}{}}C=C\overset{H}{\underset{H}{}} + H_2O$$

This is simply the reverse of "Addition of Water" to an alkene, but with different conditions. Note that for certain alcohols this reaction will produce two different products.

Reaction with Phosphorus Pentachloride:

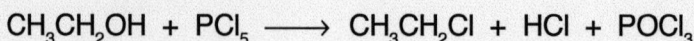

$$CH_3CH_2OH + PCl_5 \longrightarrow CH_3CH_2Cl + HCl + POCl_3$$

Reaction with Concentrated Hydrochloric Acid:

$$CH_3CH_2OH + \underset{conc}{HCl} \longrightarrow CH_3CH_2Cl + H_2O$$

Reaction with Potassium Bromide and 50% Concentrated Sulfuric Acid:

$$CH_3CH_2OH + HBr \longrightarrow CH_3CH_2Br + H_2O$$

The HBr is produced in situ by the reaction between potassium bromide and 50% concentrated sulfuric acid:

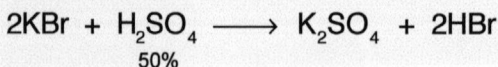

$$2KBr + \underset{50\%}{H_2SO_4} \longrightarrow K_2SO_4 + 2HBr$$

Reaction with Red Phosphorus and Iodine:

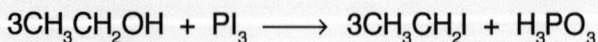

$$3CH_3CH_2OH + PI_3 \longrightarrow 3CH_3CH_2I + H_3PO_3$$

The PI_3 is produced in situ by refluxing red phosphorus with iodine:

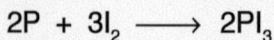

$$2P + 3I_2 \longrightarrow 2PI_3$$

15

Analytical Techniques

What do infrared spectra tell us?

What do mass spectra tell us about
elements and molecules?

Infrared Spectrum Peaks:

- Always comment on whether there is *(or is not)* an $O-H$ or $N-H$ peak in the spectrum
- Always comment on whether there is *(or is not)* a $C=O$ or $C=C$ peak in the spectrum

Use the data sheet carefully: the O—H and N—H peaks occur in similar places, and the C=O and C=C peaks occur in similar places.
These peaks will allow you to determine whether you have an alkane, alkene, amine, alcohol, aldehyde/ketone or carboxylic acid.

Mass Spectrum Peaks:

Elements:

- The number of peaks tells you how many different isotopes are present
- The m/z value of each peak indicates the relative isotopic mass
- The height of each peak tells you the relative abundance of that isotope

Molecules:

- The molecular ion (M^+) peak indicates the molecular mass of the molecule
- The other peaks tell you about the fragmentation pattern of a molecule

The M^+ peak is usually the one with the highest m/z value, but be careful not to choose the M+1 peak by mistake

16

Practical Techniques

Which apparatus and techniques do you
need to be familiar with?

What is the purpose of each?

Reflux:
The reaction mixture is continually boiled (in the flask) and condensed (in the Liebig condenser) in order to allow time for the reaction to take place without the loss of volatile compounds.

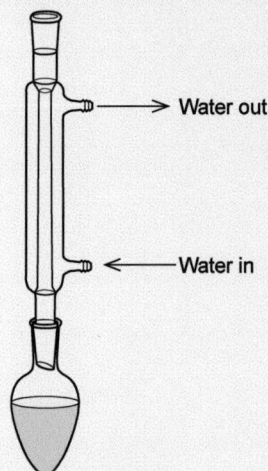

Water out

Water in

Distillation:
Liquids are separated on the basis of their boiling points, allowing a more volatile product to be separated from the reaction mixture.

Fractional distillation is used to separate useful hydrocarbon fuels from crude oil

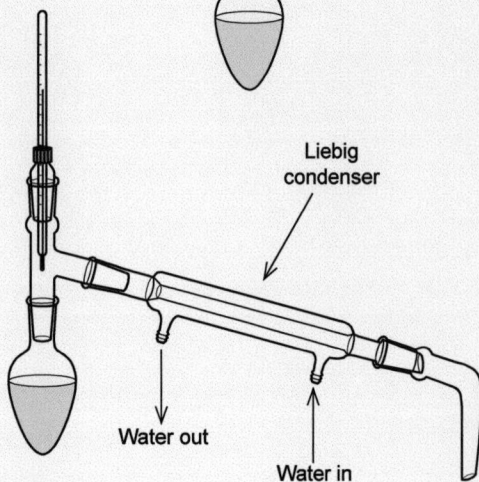

Liebig condenser

Water out

Water in

Separating funnel:
Separates an organic layer from an aqueous layer.

Drying:
An organic liquid is shaken with an anhydrous salt (e.g. $MgSO_4$ or $CaCl_2$) to remove water, then filtered to remove the drying agent.

Boiling Point Determination:
The distillation apparatus can be used to determine the boiling point of a compound by heating it slowly and recording the temperature range over which it boils. Less pure samples will boil at higher temperatures and over a wider range of temperatures.

Environmental Concerns

What 6 pollutants are produced from the combustion of fossil fuels?

What do catalytic converters do?

Name 2 alternative fuels.

Discuss the environmental issues associated with polymers, and give some solutions.

Combustion of Fossil Fuels:

Combustion produces carbon dioxide (CO_2), carbon monoxide (CO), nitrogen oxides (NO_x), sulfur oxides (SO_x), unburned hydrocarbons and carbon particulates

CO is toxic (it binds to haemoglobin in the blood, reducing the amount of oxygen that the blood can carry)

NO_x and SO_x are acidic – they produce acid rain

Catalytic Converters:

Catalytic converters convert CO, NO_x and unburned hydrocarbons into less harmful gases like H_2O, N_2 and CO_2

Alternative Fuels/Biofuels:

e.g. biodiesel (from renewable vegetable oil) and alcohols (from fermentation of sugar)

Renewable fuels only release the carbon dioxide they took out of the atmosphere when growing, so there is generally no net increase in the amount of carbon dioxide in the atmosphere (they are carbon neutral).

Polymers:

Most polymers do not biodegrade (so they end up in landfill sites)

Uses of Waste Polymers:

Waste polymers can be:

- recycled (e.g. by remoulding them into new products)
- burned to release energy (for producing electricity)
- cracked to produce monomers to use as a feedstock for new polymers

Biodegradable Polymers:

Scientists are developing polymers which decompose naturally

Toxic Gases:

Many polymers produce toxic gases (e.g. HCl) when burned

Removing Toxic Gases:

Scrubbers can be used to neutralise toxic gases before they are released into the atmosphere

Printed in Great Britain
by Amazon